ASTONS COACHES
KEMPSEY

1929 to 1980s

ASTONS COACHES

FORMERLY
H. J. ASTON & SONS
AND
L. J. ASTON

Dedication

We would like to dedicate this book to the Aston and Halford families and all the past and present employees of Astons Coaches.

Astons Coaches, Kempsey: 1929 to 1980s
Compiled by Astons of Kempsey Heritage Group

Published by Greyhound Self-Publishing 2023
Malvern, Worcestershire, United Kingdom.

Printed and bound by Aspect Design
89 Newtown Road, Malvern, Worcs. WR14 1PD
United Kingdom
Tel: 01684 561567
E-mail: allan@aspect-design.net
Website: www.aspect-design.net

All Rights Reserved.

Copyright © 2023 Astons of Kempsey Heritage Group

This book is sold subject to the condition that it shall not, by way of trade or otherwise, be lent, resold, hired out or otherwise circulated without the publisher's prior consent in any form of binding or cover other than that in which it is published and without a similar condition including this condition being imposed on the subsequent purchaser.

A copy of this book has been deposited with the British Library Board

Cover Design Copyright © 2023

ISBN: 978-1-915803-01-6

Contents

Introduction 7
A Short History of a Kempsey Coach Company 9
Early Memories 23
Change of Ownership 25
Conclusion 78

Let us introduce ourselves, from left to right,
Andy Curtis, Roy Westwood, Trevor Underwood,
Tony Brown, Pat Howes and Tony Harris.

Introduction

The idea began with a group of former Astons employees, sitting having a pleasant evening reminiscing. When someone said, all this information should be gathered and made into a book, so we started gathering photographs and memories. Many of the earlier years have been lost in time, especially wartime years and the fifties, so it is not a very concise account.

The group initially consisted of six former drivers: Pat Howes, Tony Harris, Tony Brown, Roy Westwood, Chris Johnson and Trevor Underwood. We are grateful to Levi Curtis and his son Andrew Curtis, nephews of Joe Aston, who through the family have provided us with a lot of very useful information. Also thank you to John Mudge for the use of his coach photograph albums. Since granting permission to use his photographic archive sadly John has passed away.

The first couple of years were slow going so we decided to spread our net wider by using the social media together with some information and a photograph published in the local newspaper. This resulted in some members of the Aston family becoming involved, who have also been willing to provide information. Several ex drivers have come forward with many tales, although not all of them able to be included! Many of the local villagers have provided valuable and interesting information. Terry Jones, who learned to drive a coach at Astons has provided an album of photographs of the fleet between 1968 and 1980, so this is more a photographic record with a little bit of history and possibly some memories.

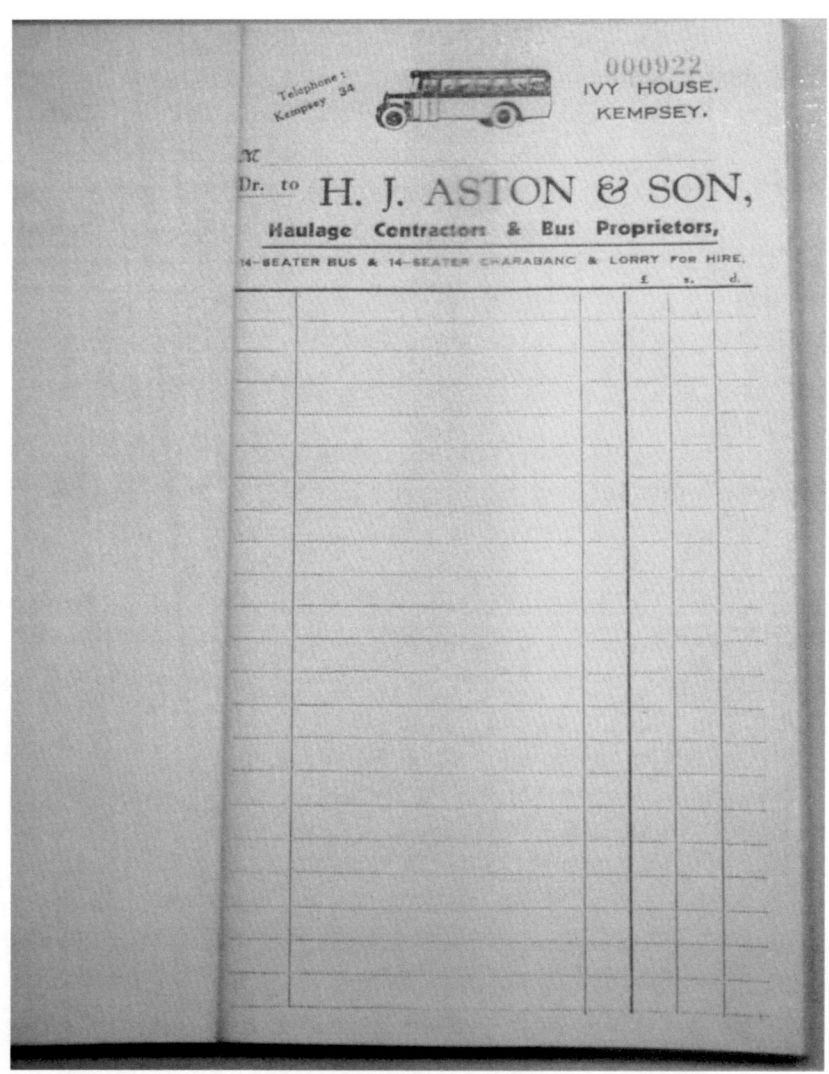

H. J. Aston receipt book from the early 1930s

A Short History of a Kempsey Coach Company

The transport business was founded in 1929, by Henry John Aston (also known locally as Jack Aston) at Ivy House in Church Street, Kempsey. Aston's was a family run business where the sons and daughters all helped in some way. He was joined by his two sons the eldest being Leonard John Aston (always known as Joe) who was the working partner in the business and Arthur Roberts Aston being the young assistant.

The company known as H. J. Aston and Sons consisted of a coach / lorry, these were very often the same chassis with removable bodies, a charabanc and later a Ford 7 car. Henry John although he started the business, he could not drive he carried on using his horse and cart leaving the driving to his sons. The lorry was often used to transport produce to local railway sidings at Defford, Pershore and local markets. They operated a 14-seater coach used for carrying children to Norton School and hop and pea pickers etc and a Ford 7 car, registration BDU 724, used to taxi people to Worcester or Upton.

Henry's wife Ellen was the one who held the business together whilst her husband was a part time village postman and helped the village undertaker.

At the age of 18 Arthur had to find an alternative living because there was not enough income in the business to support everyone financially and he was called up in 1940. During his Army Service Arthur, using his driving experience became a chauffeur to many high-ranking officers including General Alexander. Joe stayed at home running the family business which was classed a reserved occupation.

Mr and Mrs H.J. Aston

Left, Bill Bennett and right Joe Aston   Joe Aston

The coach is thought to be decorated to celebrate
King George VI coronation in 1937.

L. J. ASTON, Coach Proprietor, KEMPSEY

ANY SIZE COACHES,
ANY NUMBER, ANYWHERE!

ALL SIZE COACHES CAN BE ARRANGED FOR AT LOWEST RATES. QUOTATIONS GIVEN FREE, CARS FOR HIRE.

Private Address :—   Phone : KEMPSEY, 201.
May Cottage, Bannutt Hill. Kempsey.

S. C. ASTON, LTD.
TIMBER MERCHANTS,
TIMBERDINE AVENUE,
Tel. 4996 WORCESTER. Tel. 4996
BUYERS OF TIMBER, standing or felled. Timber is needed urgently for government purposes. We shall be pleased to offer you controlled prices.

Mrs. J. A. THOMAS & SONS,
Bakers & Confectioners,

Noted for High-class Bread.   **KEMPSEY.**

Your Patronage respectfully solicited.

FOR THE LARGEST ASSORTMENT AND BEST VALUE IN
LADIES' AND CHILDEN'S WEAR,
GENERAL DRAPERY
AND OUTFITTING

The Oldest & Best House in the City
Established over 100 years

GO TO
RUSSELL & DORRELL'S
(DRAPERS) LTD.
17 to 21, HIGH ST., WORCESTER.
AND PUMP STREET,

THE ORIGINAL STORES.
THE KEMPSEY GENERAL EMPORIUM
H. A QUARMBY & Co.
(H. A. QUARMBY)
TRY US FOR
VALUE—QUALITY—VARIETY.

OUR MOTTO.—" We are here to serve you "
Home-made Ices a Speciality.
Telephone—Kempsey 263.

"Lily of the Valley"
JUVENILE ODDFELLOWS FRIENDLY SOCIETY, M.U.
Established 1884   No. 1029 Worcs.

Children admitted from Birth. For the sum of 1d. per week members are entitled to Medical attendance and medicine when necessary.
MEETINGS Every FOUR Weeks (not fortnightly). The Old School, Kempsey.
Hours 7 p.m.—8 p.m.
CALL FOR PARTICULARS.

H. P. SMITH,
Shoeing & General Smith,

DRAYCOTT FORGE,
KEMPSEY.

All Orders Promptly Executed.

L. J. Aston advertisement taken from Kempsey Parish Magazine published in September 1944.

Joe then took over the business and operated it as L. J. Aston, still operating from Ivy House though he, his wife and young family John and Beryl lived at May Cottage, Bannut Hill, Kempsey. In 1945, the family then moved to a bungalow at 4, Church Street, Kempsey and consisted of a yard which was a former coal yard which could accommodate his vehicles.

Joe with his first coach GE 6057 in the name of L. J. Aston.
Photo taken in Main Road, Kempsey

In 1946 Mr and Mrs Aston's son John joined the business, not driving but mainly carrying out office duties along with his sister Beryl who also helped in the office. The business name then changed for a while to L. J. Aston and Son until sadly John passed away in 1948 after a tragic accident. The business name then reverted to L. J. Aston.

By this time, the lorry had long gone so the work consisted of coach work, including factory and school contract runs.

Prior to the war he operated a contract for Morganite Crucible at their Norton Factory, which was always known as the 'Jam Factory '. They made crucibles and containers out of carbon black. He operated two coaches; the contracts still being operated in the 1970s by the new business owner.

During the war he operated services on behalf of the Ministry to Pershore Airfield and to the Army Barracks at Norton, operated a late Saturday night service from Worcester to Norton Barracks on which he took a helper because the troops often became a 'little' merry. He also ran a coach transporting the men and women from Upton Upon Severn to work in the munition's factory at Blackpole, Worcester.

During the 1940s and 1950s Joe operated a fleet of Bedford O.B, W.T.B and O.W.B coaches. Photo line up taken in the yard 4, Church Street, Kempsey. 1948.

Left to right

ENP 145 Bedford OWB, Duple B32F. Purchased new 1945 and later sold to Black & White, Harvington.

DCJ 372 Bedford OWB, Duple B30F. New in 1945. Purchased from Tummery, South Wales and later sold in 1958.

EAB 545 Bedford OWB

FAB 930 Bedford OWB, Mulliner Body, B30F. Purchased new in 1946 and sold July 1957.

BUN 709 Bedford WTB, Duple C26F. New in 1939 and later sold and becoming a mobile café.

FNP 411 Bedford OB, Duple C29F. Purchased new in 1947 and later sold in 1952.

Fred Edwards pictured with HNP 27 Bedford OB, Duple C29F. Purchased new in 1949 and sold in 1962.

HNP 114 Bedford OB. Photo taken at Elmley Castle, Pershore. Sold as a mobile shop in March 1962.

Post war L.J. Aston not only offered coach hire but a taxi service and wedding car hire. Joe was always proud of his vehicles especially the cars which were his pride and joy. All Joe's personal cars were used as wedding cars, taxi's and sometimes funeral cars. One of the cars to stand out and used as a wedding car was a gold and blue Vauxhall Cresta registration number RDD 1. It was used by family members and many local villagers on their wedding day. His other cars were numerous Austin's among them CYB 256, FK 8040, CVP 724.

Vauxhall Cresta RDD 1 leaving Old St Peters Church, King St, Worcester, April 30th, 1960.

Joe Aston

During Joe's ownership, driver's duties, in the early days not only involved driving and maintaining his vehicles but was to take one of the taxis and a trailer loaded with feed and water to his cows which were kept in a field next to Kempsey Church. They also helped look after the pigs which he kept at the yard. He also provided the drivers as pallbearers to the local Undertaker which was Mr A.T. Jeynes.

At the rear of the yard was an orchard where the Kempsey Baptist Chapel held their fetes every year. Joe was very involved with the Chapel always providing coaches for Sunday school outings and evening mystery tours.

By 1951 Joe was operating six coaches, when he purchased a new Bedford SB with a Duple, 33-seater body KNP 186 and was painted silver and blue, a new colour. Trevor Underwood a Kempsey lad who later became one of Joe's drivers and then in the late 1970s became Transport Manager for Astons, can remember travelling on this coach to see a Pantomime at Malvern Theatre when he was six years old and traveling in the single seat alongside the driver.

Later in the 1950s Joe purchased the business of Downes Coaches of Droitwich Road, Worcester (the premises now being a tyre fitting company). This came with a fairly new Bedford SB, 41-seater Duple coach NFK 107 along with its driver from Downes, Doug Hanson who was now employed by Joe.

During the 1950s and 1960s the fleet was gradually updated to Bedford S.Bs with Duple Vega Bodies.

KNP 186

One of the first Bedford SBs built, Duple Vega C33F, Chassis No 4688. New to Mr Aston in 1951. It was the company's longest serving vehicle, still in Kempsey early 1974.

Photo taken on Sidbury Carpark, Worcester, 26th July 1965

NDG 231

Bedford SB, Duple Bodied C33F.

New in 1954 to Yeomans purchased by Mr Aston in 1958 and sold on to G. P. Smith of St Georges, January 1967.

Photo taken on Sidbury Carpark, Worcester, 5th September 1965

KBU 96

Bedford SB, Duple Bodied C33F.

New in 1954 to Hanmer of Wrexham, sold to Midwales Motorways of Newtown in September 1960 and later purchased by Mr Aston.

Photo taken in Deansway, Worcester, 10th October 1964

NFK 107

Bedford SBG, Chassis No40749, Duple Vega C41F.

New to Downes, Worcester in 1956 and later purchased by Mr Aston in May 1960. It was scrapped in 1968.

Photo taken on 'The Goodrest' public house carpark, Worcester, 7th November 1964

SOL 279

Bedford SBG, chassis No 41099, Duple Vega, C41F.

New to Yarringtons of Eardiston in 1956. Purchased by Mr Aston in January 1966 and sold to Powell of Tarrington in October 1969.

Photo taken on Copenhagen Street Carpark, Worcester, 17th June 1966

SDD 461

Bedford SBG, chassis No 48780 Duple Vega, C41F.

New in 1956 to Gilletts of Winchcombe. Purchased by Mr Aston in 1962 and sold to Evans and Wood of Shifnal in 1971.

Photo taken in Happy Land, Bromyard Road, Worcester, 25th October 1964

XDG 283

Bedford SB3, chassis No70366, Duple Super Vega, C41F.

New in 1959 to Nash & Cox, Coleford. Purchased by Mr Aston in June 1963. After serving with Astons this coach was sold to a Worcester based speedway group as a non-PSV. In 1977 it was used by Travelways Taxis of Worcester for use as an office and storeroom.

Photo taken in Lich Street, Worcester, 21st July 1963

WNT 48

Bedford SB3, chassis No 86823 Duple Super Vega, C41F.

New in 1961 to Foxhall of Bridgenorth. Purchased by Mr Aston in 1967 and was the most recent purchase to be passed into the ownership of the Halford family.
Converted to a mobile caravan by March 1974.

Photo taken at Aston's Yard, Church Street, Kempsey, 5th March 1967

L. J. ASTON COACH PROPRIETOR
KEMPSEY
Tel.: Kempsey 201

ANY SIZE COACHES
NY WHERE
NY NUMBER

Taxis for Hire
Quotations given Free
Private Parties Catered for

G. W. HALFORD
The Stores, Kempsey

A full selection of HIGH CLASS GOODS at Town Prices

Orders Delivered   'Phone: Kempsey 263

H. R. THOMAS   MOTOR ENGINEER

SUNNYSIDE GARAGE
KEMPSEY   Repairs of every description
                       Complete Overhauls
'Phone: Kempsey 310

S. J. CLARKE   REG'D. PLUMBING AND
                    HEATING CONTRACTOR

"WESTBOURNE," KINGS HILL, KEMPSEY

Pumps & Sanitary Installations : Central & Domestic Heating

Estimates Free   'Phone: Kempsey 393

R. D. PATRICK   (Successor to A. T. Jeynes)

NORTOFT, 40, MAIN ROAD, KEMPSEY

Decorator and Carpenter, etc.   General House Repairs
Coffin Maker and Undertaker.   Cremations
Estimates Free   **Tel. 444**

Cover picture by D. G. North: West Wycombe from Church Hill

L.J. Aston advertisement taken from Kempsey Parish Magazine, published in October 1961.

A few of Joe's drivers some fulltime and part time up to 1968 are remembered as listed below: -

Bill Edwards	Bill Bennett
Dick Gage	Bern Wiggins
Tom Wiggins	Jack Fessey
Doug Fessey	Roll Chandler
Doug Hanson	Ted Hanson
Arthur Price	Trevor Underwood
Bill Hayes	Fred Edwards
Archie Glover	Phil Shuck
Harry Sanders	Edwin Keyte
Sid Rowberry	Tom Clee *(wages clerk)*
Tom Symmonds	Joe Higham

Early Memories

Post war, Kempsey School use to walk to the local parish hall for lunch, also to the Lawns Pool for swimming lessons. When it rained Joe was hired to take the children to the Hall for lunch but never to the pool.

Beryl Griffin, Joe's daughter remembered the weather of 1947 and Dr Dorothy Terry getting stuck in a snow drift along Pixham Ferry Lane, her father sent his drivers to dig her car out of the snow. Beryl passed away August 2018.

Mr and Mrs Bull can remember that Astons ran a works bus from Upton Upon Severn and through to Kempsey running into the old Providence Works, Worcester which was part of the Metal Box and returning at night, this operated from 1952 until 1957 and may have run before and after these dates.

Joy Clee recalls her father, Mr Edwin Keyte a local Joiner and Wheelwright, during the war, often drove for Joe when he was short of drivers.

Levi Curtis Joe's nephew remembers in the 1940s getting up early in the school holidays at his home at Ivy House and going with the drivers to pick up the hop pickers and take them to the local hop picking fields and often went with the drivers down to the Ford in Kempsey known as 'The Rocky' to wash their coaches. He also helped out taxi driving and remembers in the late 1950s Joe had a taxi contract every Sunday morning to pick up Lord Dudley from his home at Baynhall, Kempsey and take him to Foregate Street Station. He recalls his father Sam Curtis and his Uncle, Bill Bennett who were both brother in-laws of Joe excavating by hand for the yard's petrol tank at 4, Church Street.

Levi's Aunty Ethel, Joe's wife organised everything in Joe's absence and rang him on many occasions to carry out a taxi job for them if Joe was not available to do so.

Mrs Beryl Gummery who was a cousin of Joe's remembers Aston's transporting the older girls and boys from Kempsey School to Upton Upon Severn for cookery classes and woodwork classes. This was also remembered by Mrs Doris Francis who was at Kempsey School at the same time as Beryl. She thought it must have been in the late 1930s and 1940s. Both these ladies are over 90 years old.

Joan Chambers remembers her mother Joan Clark, who was the treasurer of Kempsey Cornflower club and with Mrs Flo Sears organised day trips to various locations including Windsor, Weston Super Mare, Alton Towers, Trentham Gardens. In the early years, the shorter journeys would often be in a wooden seated bus.

Jack Bray, Joe's nephew, remembers in the 1940s to the 1950s travelling from Kempsey Village to Stanley Road School where there would be three other coaches transporting children from local areas to the school. Jacks brother Fred often used his art and design skills to help Joe with the brown and cream livery design used on the coaches during the 40s and 50s.

Many people remember travelling on Astons Coaches to Kempsey County Primary School from Stonehall, Pirton and Kerswell Green areas. In the 1960s L.J. Aston started operating a school bus from Kempsey to The Hill Secondary Modern School, Upton Upon Severn.

A little story about my Uncle, Roll Chandler

One very foggy night way back my uncle was making his way back to Kempsey after a job. He lived with his mum and dad at "Chandlers Cottage", Kerswell Green. This cottage still exists albeit a new building.

Well he must have been out early the next day, so he decided to take the bus home. Unbeknown to him a Kempsey resident saw the bus and my Uncle, and thought, "I can't see a thing, I'll follow the bus back to the yard".

Well Roll drove back to Kerswell Green parked the bus in the lane next to the cottage and climbed out.

"Where am we Roll?" said the puzzled follower "Well I'm Home I don't know about you".

I used to know the name of the person, but it's slipped my memory.

Alan Chandler

Roll Chandler pictured with BUN 709 Duple Bodied Bedford WTB. Sold as a mobile café.

Change of Ownership

By now Joe was operating six coaches when he decided to retire on the 31st December 1967 and sell the business to Mr and Mrs G.W. Halford, known as Bill and Chris, who owned the Original Stores, Church Street next to the yard.

Joe moved out of the bungalow at the yard and into a new bungalow, which he had built by a local builder, Clee & Sons Ltd.

The coaches still operated from the yard with Arthur Price driver / mechanic moving into the bungalow. For the first year he with the assistance of Trevor Underwood ran the business until Chris and Bill's son, Tony, returned from Canada where he had been teaching, to run the business.

The business had a solid base of schools and work contracts supplemented by private hire trips. An enthusiastic and innovative work force led to the company becoming a leading player in all local activities. School sports, culture and swimming journeys were an area of significant growth. Continental tours were in their infancy but, with an enthusiastic young staff, became the route of expansion in the late 70's and 80's. Work was undertaken for many firms taking adults and school parties to all parts of Europe, including express services to Poland for the national carrier Euro lines.

In 1980 a new arm of the firm was created, Ski Astons, which created much needed winter work to Austria and Switzerland. The schools tour company, Ultima Travel was acquired by the company in 1990. Under the banner of "Astons Holidays" trips were organised to most parts of Europe as well as the UK.

Although very successful, the industry came under increased pressure from cheap airlines in the 90's and the millennium. This forced a new sense of direction and the company moved into the service bus sector. This proved to be an incredibly positive move and the need to expand led to the company moving to a new location at Clerkenleap in 1997.

The following photos show some of the buses and coaches that passed through 'Astons' under the ownership of the Halford family and how front line coaches became more luxurious and were updated on a regular basis to keep up with the changes and demands of the industry.

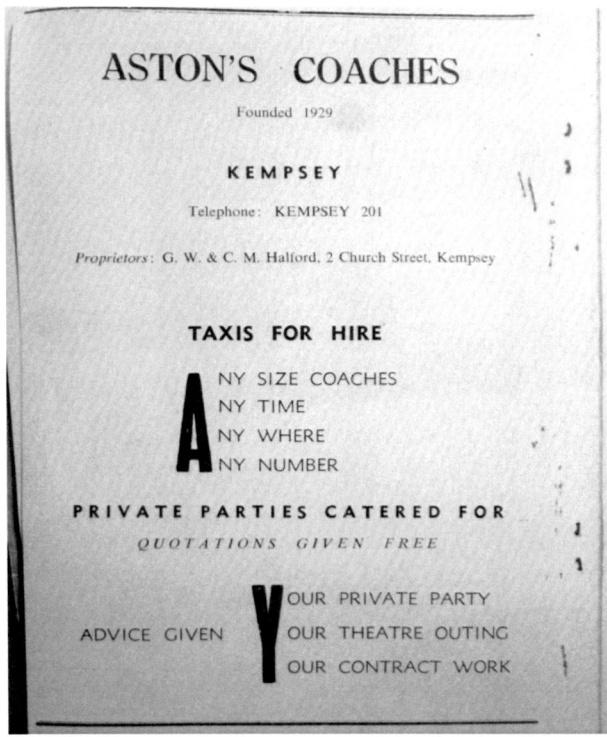

Astons Coaches advertisement taken from Kempsey Parish Magazine published in May 1970 with the new proprietors G.W. & C.M. Halford.

382 BLD

Bedford SB8. Chassis NO 86298 (powered by a Leyland engine), Harrington Crusader, CF41 bodied.

This was the Halfords family's first purchase and was an ex – Grey-Green of London coach which arrived in June 1968 from Barry's Coaches of Morton – in – Marsh. It is not known when it was withdrawn from service.

Photo is taken at Pitchcroft Road, Worcester, 26th September 1969

WDU 817

Commer Avenger IV. Chassis NO 94A 0213, Plaxton, CF41 bodied.

This Commer was purchased from Stan Fox of Worcester in May 1969 and was sold to Naylor of Halesworth in July 1970.

Photo taken 27th January 1968

ORD 250

Bedford SB3. Chassis No56357 Duple Vega bodied, C41F.

Purchased in June 1969 from Smiths of Reading. It was later sold onto Sergeant of Kington in March 1971.

Photo taken 1st November 1969

VHL 933

Bedford SB5. Chassis No 90165. Plaxton Embassy bodied, C41F.

Purchased in August 1969 from Jones of Frome. This coach was the last of its type to be operated by Astons. It was originally No 933 in the West Riding fleet in Yorkshire. It left Astons 10th October 1977 to Everton of Droitwich.

Photo taken 27th September 1969

CEF 717D

Bedford VAM5, Chassis No6809844. Plaxton Panorama bodied, C45F.

This was an ex- Bee-line of Middlesbrough coach and was purchased in May 1970 by Astons and ran until July 1971. It was then operated by Price of Bishop's Castle in Shropshire.

KDF 851E

Bedford VAS1.Chassis No 7838542, Plaxton Embassy, C29F bodied.

This coach was purchased in May 1970 from B.E.W. Beavis (Alpine Tours) of Bussage, near Stroud, Gloucester. The coach remained with Astons until 17th July 1972 and then operated by Stigwoods of High Wycombe, Buckinghamshire.

Photo taken on Pitchcroft Carpark, Worcester, 24th March 1971

ASTONS COACHES
(Prop.: G. W. and C. M. HALFORD)
KEMPSEY, NR. WORCESTER
Telephone: WORCESTER 820201

GO "CONTINENTAL"
IN OUR LUXURY PORTUGUESE 53-SEATER COACH

Other luxury coaches available from 29 seats

LET US HELP TO ARRANGE YOUR

OUTINGS — DAY TOURS — THEATRE TRIPS

BRITISH AND CONTINENTAL COACHING HOLIDAYS

ALL ENQUIRIES AND ESTIMATES WITHOUT OBLIGATION

Astons Coaches advertisement taken from Kempsey Parish Magazine published in August 1973.

EWP699C

Bedford SB5, Chassis No 96578 Plaxton Panorama, C41F.

This coach came from Yarranton of Eardiston, Tenbury Wells in April 1971. It was with Astons until June 1972, when it was sold to Austin of Aston Diddlebury, near Craven Arms.

Photo taken Croft Road Carpark, Worcester, 29th May 1971

CVJ 800C

Bedford Val 14, Chassis No 1568 Duple Midland, B52F.

This bus came from Yeoman of Canon Pyon in July 1972 and operated with Astons until 29th December 1976, when it was sold on to Bryn Morgan of Monmouth.

Photo taken at Lowesmoor, Worcester, 8th October 1972

OVU 858H

Bedford Val 70, Chassis No 472724 Caetano Estoril, C53F.

This Portuguese bodied coach arrived from Stubbs of Manchester in 1971 and was with Astons until 1973 when it was sold to Glynne of Glasgow.

Photo taken at Croft Road Carpark, Worcester, 1st July 1972

FTC 330J

Bedford SB5, Chassis No 486497, Plaxton Panorama, C41F.

Purchased 4th August 1972 from Grange of Morecambe. This was the last 'SB' to enter Astons fleet. It was sold on 14th December 1972 to Hambridge of Kidlington and later passed to Andy's Coaches of Birmingham.

Photo taken at Astons Yard, Kempsey, 29th December 1972

CVJ500C
Bedford Val 14, Chassis number 1614, Plaxton Panorama C52F.

This coach was purchased in September 1970 and was the largest coach the company owned at this time. It came from Yeoman of Canon Pyon, Hereford. In October 1974 it was sold on to L.W. Phillips of Leamington Spa.

UDF 201H
Bedford VAS5, Chassis No478620, Plaxton Panorama IV C29F.

After KDF851E the company's other 29-seater coach was purchased 12th September 1972. This coach also came from B.E.W. Beavis of Bussage. It was sold to J.W. Camplin & Sons of Donnington, Lincolnshire, 11th June 1975.

SNP 700L
Ford R226, Chassis No BCO4LU57521 Duple Dominant, C53F
This new coach arrived 30th January 1973 and ran until 2nd December 1974, when it passed to Edwards of Markham. It later moved to Croft of Cardiff.

Photo taken at Astons Yard, Kempsey, 18th February 1973

NCK 347
Leyland Atlantean PDR1/1, Chassis No590987, MCW, H44/34F Metro Cammel.
This was the company's first double decker bus and was an ex Ribble Atlantean, their fleet no.1606. It arrived at Astons 6th August 1972 and gave good service, mainly on school contracts until it was withdrawn from service for scrap on 5th September 1979.

Photo taken at Astons Yard, Kempsey

GTG 637K

Seddon Pennine VI, Chassis No 48441 Duple Viceroy, C57F.

This was Astons first 12 metre coach and arrived 14th June 1973, from S.A.Bebb of Llantwit Fardre, South Wales. It was sold in February 1974 to Midland Travel of Coventry.

Photo taken Sansome Walk, Worcester

YAB 600M

Bedford YRQ, Chassis No 453170, Duple Dominant, C45F.

On 4th January 1974 this new coach came into service. This coach served for approximately one year and in December 1974 was sold to Evans of Senghenydd, South Wales. It later moved onto Parfitt's of Rhymney.

Photo taken at Astons Yard, Kempsey, 24th January 1974

Astons Coaches advertisement taken from Kempsey Parish News published in 1974

MTX 948L

A.E.C. Reliance 691, Chassis No6U3ZR-23348,
Plaxton Panorama Elite III, C49F.

This coach came from Edwards of Beddau in March 1974. It only ran until July of that year when it was sold to Alec Head of Lutton, Cambridgeshire.

Photo taken at Astons Yard, Kempsey, 7th April 1974

AWP 400M

Volvo B58-66, Chassis No4555 Duple Dominant, C57F.

This was the company's first Volvo and was delivered 26th April 1974. On 11th February 1976 it was sold to R.A.Price (Excelsior Coachways) of Wrockwardine Wood, Telford. It later returned from R.A.Price on 14th June 1977 and was soon re painted white with orange lettering. It was sold again 16th August 1979 to Densley & Bennett (Cliff's Coaches) of Bath.

TBD 97G

Ford R226, Chassis NoBCO4JU53143, Duple Viceroy, C53F.

Originally with Yorks Travel of Cogenhoe, Northampton and came to Astons in June 1974 from R.S.Bosworth of Worcester. It was sold to Justice Travel of Daventry in March 1976 and later to Ralph Garrett of Leicester.

Photo taken in Sansome Walk, Worcester, 15th September 1973

447 CWK

A.E.C. Reliance 470 Chassis No 2MU4RA5452, Plaxton Panorama, C41F.

This coach came from Silverline of Hounslow to Astons in December 1974. In 1976 it was sold to Ken Shorthouse (KCS Tours) of Cutnall Green, near Droitwich.

Photo taken in Sansome Walk, Worcester

DRU 245L

Ford 226, Chassis No BCO4MY64219, Plaxton Panorama Elite III, C53F.

Purchased on 6th November 1974 from Excelsior European Motorways of Bournemouth. It was with Astons until March 1975 when it was then sold to Raff of Gravesend, Kent.

ANW 710C

A.E.C. Reliance 470, Chassis No 2MU3RA5504, Roe C37F.

It was purchased new in 1965 by Leeds City Transport. It was later sold on to Hudson of Cottingham, near Hull. On the 9th January 1975 it arrived at Astons Yard and was used extensively on school contracts until it was sold in March 1984.

Photo taken at Astons yard March 1980

HWP 172N

Ford R1114, Chassis No BCO4MS55269, Caetano Estoril II, C53F.

Purchased new on December 1974 and was with the company until 1st October 1975 when it was sold to Peachkarn of Chessington, Surrey. It later moved on to Crook's Coaches of Booker, near High Wycombe.

Photo taken in Battenhall Road, Worcester, 19th April 1975

HWP 173N

Bedford YRQ, Chassis No EW451327, Duple Dominant, C45F.

This coach was purchased new and entered service 8th January 1975. Later that year it was sold to Johnson of Rushden, Northants. It was later sold to Fale's Coaches of Combe Down, near Bath.

Photo taken in London Road, Worcester, April 1975

KAB 400N

Volvo B58-56, Chassis No 6701 Duple Dominant Express, C53F.
Purchased new and entered service 25th March 1975.

Photo taken at Astons Yard, Kempsey, 18th November 1979

GNK 599G

Ford R226, Chassis No BCO4HY59212 Plaxton Panorama Elite, C53F.
This coach was purchased 16th June 1975 from Fingland of Manchester. It was originally with Draper of Luton.
On the 22nd June 1976 it was sold to Hunt of Alford.

Photo taken in Sansome Walk, Worcester

FTB 824J

Ford R192, Chassis No BCO4KA46536 Duple Viceroy, C36F.

This coach was purchased 11th June 1975 from Hilliard of Accrington, Lancs. It was sold on 3rd May 1976 and in July 1977 it moved on to Smith & Rees of Rhigos, near Aberdare.

Photo taken in Sansome Walk, Worcester

OWP 24P

Ford R1114, Chassis NoBCO4RC55496 Duple Dominant, C53F.

This coach entered service in January 1976 and ran until November of the same year. It was then sold to Mitchell Compact of Crawley, West Sussex.

OWP 25P

Caetano integral, C45F, with Bedford YRQ running units. Chassis No 452745.

An experimental rear-engine Bedford coach. This coach was purchased new 8th January 1976. Caetano built just seven of these YRQ integrals. This one was sold on October 14th of that year to Lawson's Coaches of Methven, near Perth, Scotland.

WNC 16L

Ford R192. Chassis NoBCO4MR59791 Duple Dominant, C45F.

This coach arrived 5th May 1976 from Fingland of Manchester. It was sold 12th August that year to E.H Thorne & Son (Pewsey Vale Coaches) of Pewsey, Wiltshire.

OWP 23P
Bedford YRQ, Chassis No 454327 Duple Dominant, C45F.
Purchased new on 4th October 1975. This coach ran with Astons until 14th October 1976. It was then sold to Dolphin Coaches of Poole, Dorset.

Photo taken at Astons Yard, Kempsey, April 1976

PUT 153M
Caetano integral, C45F, with Bedford YRQ running units.
Chassis No 474629.
This identical twin to OWP 25P was not new to Astons. It was originally the Moseley 'YRQ integral demonstrator. It came to Astons 10th February 1976 from Bywater of Rochdale. It was sold on the 14th October 1976 to Larry Stephenson of Ryhope, Sunderland.

Photo taken at Astons Yard, Kempsey

PUY 794P

Volvo B58-61, Chassis No 7561 Duple Dominant, C57F.

Purchased new 17th February 1976. It left the fleet 1st July 1978 when it spent a year with Rowson Bros, of Hayes, Middlesex. It returned to Astons, Kempsey in the early summer of 1979.

Photo taken in Wylds Lane, Worcester. (Driver, Trevor Underwood)

88 RTO

Daimler CRG6 Fleetline, Chassis No60266 Northern Counties, H44/33F.

Originally Nottingham City Transport 88. This bus came to Astons 12th April 1976 and was in service until 30th January 1979 when it was then sold to Sykes (scrap dealer) of Barnsley.

Photo taken at Astons yard, Kempsey

EBW 661K

A.E.C. Reliance 691, Chassis No6U3ZR57755 Caetano Lisboa, C57F.

This coach came to Astons from Mayo of Caterham in April 1976. It had been new to Hambridge of Kidlington, Oxford, then taken over by Heyfordian. On 14th October 1976 it left Astons and was sold to Edwards of Joys Green, Lydbrook, Forest of Dean.

Photo taken at Astons Yard, Kempsey

VAB 557R

Ford R1114, Chassis NoBCO4SB68562 Caetano Estoril II, C53F.

This coach was purchased new 17th September 1976 and was sold 24th October 1977. In April 1978 it was in service with Heron of Salford, Manchester.

Photo taken at Astons Yard, Kempsey

UUY 786R

Ford R1014, Chassis No BCO4RP65386 Plaxton Supreme, C45F.

It was purchased new 12th August 1976 and entered service immediately. It stayed with Astons until 20th October 1977 when it was sold to Barry's Coaches of Weymouth.

Photo taken in Edgar Street, Worcester

WNP 986R

Ford R1114, Chassis NoBCO4RM64769 Plaxton Supreme, C53F.

This coach was used by Plaxtons in their advertisements for their 'Supreme' coach body. It was delivered new to Astons 29th October 1976 and entered service in January 1977. It was later sold on 15th November 1977 to Greenway Travel of Hitchen, Hertfordshire.

WNP 861R

Ford R1114, Chassis No BCO4SB68927 Duple Dominant, C53F.

This coach was delivered new in July 1976 and was named 'Sabrina Superb' but did not enter service until January 1977. It was sold 19th December 1977 to Edwards of Markham.

VUY 446R

Ford R1114, Chassis No BCO4SB68563 Caetano Estoril II.

This coach was identical to VAB 557R and arrived new at Astons 15th October 1976. It was sold 5th January 1978 and later purchased by Heron of Salford in April 1978.

Photo taken October 1976 at Astons Yard, Kempsey

Ford, Duple bodied, GSN 500E, Astons Yard, Kempsey.
Absorbed into the fleet of Astons from the purchase of Bosworth Coaches, London Road, Worcester, March 1977.

YAB 416R

Bedford YMT, Chassis No 3DZOFW454308 Duple Dominant II, C53.
Purchased new on 8th April 1977 and ran in plain white until 1st June of that year. It was then sold to W.F.C.& H.G. Taylor of Sutton Scotney, near Winchester.

Photo taken at Astons Yard, Kempsey

GHA 334D

Leyland Leopard PSU4/4R, Chassis NoL61413, Plaxton Panorama, C40F.

Originally Midland Red 'LC9' class 5834. The coach came from the National Bus Company on the 14th July 1977. It was with Aston's until the 1st December 1978 when it was sold to Everton Goldliner Coaches of Droitwich.

Photo taken at Aston's Yard, Kempsey

GHA 333D

Leyland Leopard PSU4/4R, Chassis NoL61412, Plaxton Panorama, C45F.

Originally Midland Red 5833. The coach was identical to GHA 334D as a 40 seater coach. It arrived at Aston's 15th July 1977 and re-seated into a 45 seater. It was sold along with GHA 334D to Everton Goldliner Coaches of Droitwich.

Photo taken at Aston's yard

VUO 787J

Leyland Leopard, Chassis No 7100166 Caetano Lisboa, C51F.

This coach was new to Trathens of Yelverton, Devon. It came from South Wales Police 1st April 1977 and ran until 25th June 1977 when it was then sold to Fullarton of Falkirk, Scotland.

Photo taken in Warndon, Worcester

KBB266D

Leyland PDR1/1 Atlantean, Chassis NoL62424 Alexander H44/34F.

Previously 1466 in the Tyne and Wear PTE fleet this bus was purchased by Astons 4th July 1977 and was used for school contracts.

Photo taken at Astons Yard, Kempsey, May 1978

ONK 645H

Leyland Leopard PSU3A/4R, Chassis No 7000288, Plaxton Panorama Elite, C48F.

Purchased from Grey - Green of London 23rd May 1977 and ran with Astons until 5th January 1978 when it was sold to Len Munden & Son (Empress Coaches) of Bristol.

Photo taken in Astons Yard, Kempsey, May 1977

DWP 2S
Volvo B58 – 61, Chassis No9481, Plaxton Supreme.
This coach was collected from Plaxtons 4th January 1978.

Photo taken at Astons Yard, Kempsey

DWP 3S
A.E.C. Reliance 691 Chassis No 6U3ZR 33562, Plaxton Supreme, C53F.
This coach was also collected from Plaxtons 4th January 1978 and ran with Astons until 11th April of that year when it was then sold to Taylor's of Sutton Scotney.

Photo taken at Astons Yard, Kempsey

DWP 4S

Ford R1114, Chassis NoBCO4SL63634 Duple Dominant I, C53F, with a continental step to the rear exit door.

This new coach arrived on 25th October 1977 and ran until 21st December 1978. It was then sold to Brough (Whippet Coaches) of Wimborne, Dorset.

Photo taken at Astons yard, Kempsey, December 1977

DWP 5S

Ford R1014, Chassis NoBCO4ST60645 Plaxton Supreme, C45F.

This 45-seater was purchased new on 15th November 1977 and was a replacement for UUY 786R. It was sold on 16th October 1978 to G.H.Watts of Leicester.

Photo taken Astons Yard, Kempsey, December 1977

DWP 6S

Bedford YMT, Chassis NoGW455112 Van Hool McArdle 300-line, C53F.

This coach was collected new from Moseley's of Loughborough on 15th December 1977 and was named 'Lady Christina'. It was sold on 16th October 1978 to Roger Garrett of Newton Abbot.

Photo taken at Bromyard Road, Worcester

DWP 7S

Ford R1114, Chassis NoBCO4SL63861 Duple Dominant I, C53F.

This coach was purchased new on 13th September 1977 and was with the company until 17th July 1978. It was named 'Sabrina 2', replacing WNP 861R being named 'Sabrina'. It then passed to Plant's Coaches of Gnosall, Staffordshire.

Photo taken at Astons Yard, Kempsey, December 1977

GNP 313S

Volvo B58-56, Chassis No9684 Caetano Lisboa II, C53F.

This coach was purchased on 25th May 1978 and was still with the company on 31st December 1979.

Photo taken at Bromyard Road, Worcester

DNT 556L

Leyland Leopard, Chassis No 7300711 Caetano Lisboa II Express, C53F.

This coach was purchased from Eagle Coachways of Telford on 4th May 1978 and was in service with the company until 8th September 1978 when it then purched by Dougalls Coaches of Dundee.

Photo taken at Croft Road Car Park, Worcester

HRU 713N

Ford R1014, Chassis No BCO4PG68420 Plaxton Panorama Elite, C45F.

This was the only remaining Ford R-series coach remaining in the current fleet at the date of 31st December 1979. It was purchased from Excelsior of Bournemouth.

Photo taken at Bromyard Road, Worcester, December 1979

TJH 366M

Volvo B58-61, Chassis No 4874 Plaxton Panorama Elite, C50F.

This was one of a pair of coaches, with consecutive chassis numbers purchased in December 1978 from Diadem of St Albans, Herts.

Photo taken at Astons Yard, Kempsey

VNK 879M

Volvo B58-60, Chassis No4873 Plaxton Panorama Elite, C50F.

This is the other twin coach purchased in December 1978 from Diadem of St Albans, Herts. Re-registered to RDU 4 in June 1982.

Photo taken Bromyard Road, Worcester

TGD 2R

Volvo B58-61, Chassis No 6824 Plaxton Viewmaster, C57F.

This was an ex-coach from Parks of Hamilton and was purchased in December 1978, named 'Astons Euro-Glide'.

Photo taken at Astons Yard, Kempsey, 21st October 1979

JAB 5T

Volvo B58-56, Chassis No 10395 Plaxton Supreme, C53F.

Purchased new in January 1979, the livery was designed with red based bands to match JAB 8T which had blue bands.

Photo taken at Astons Yard, Kempsey, August 1980

JAB 8T

Volvo B58-56, Chassis No 10390 Plaxton Supreme, C53F.
This Volvo coach was purchased new in October 1978.

Photo taken at Astons Yard, Kempsey, August 1980

JAB 7T

Bedford YMT, Chassis No 456084 Van Hool 300-line, C53F. This coach was purchased new on 17th August 1978 and named, 'Lord William'. It was identical to DWP 6S and was sold 13th December 1979.

Photo taken at Bromyard Road, Worcester

ETN 99C

Leyland Atlantean, Chassis No 40607. Weymann, H44/34F.

This Atlantean came from Tyne and Wear and arrived at Astons on 21st March 1979 and was used as most of the other double decker's in the fleet for school and college contracts.

Photo taken at Astons Yard, Kempsey, March 1980

TGD 991R

Volvo B58-56, Chassis No7869 Plaxton Viewmaster, C53F.

This was another Viewmaster from Parks of Hamilton and was purchased on 20th 1979. It spent the summer of that year on lone to Everton Goldliner Coaches of Droitwich.

Photo taken at Droitwich Town Centre

DSJ 302V

Volvo B58-61 Van Hool Alizee.

This coach was a demonstrator for Volvo until 1981 when it then became one of Astons fleet. It was sold in August 1983 to Giles of Dobwalls.

Photo taken at Astons Yard, Kempsey

TNP 6V

Volvo B58-61, Caetano Alpha.

This coach was purchased new in January 1980 and was sold to Ffoshelig in March 1984.

Photo taken at Astons Yard, Kempsey, September 1980

TNP 9V

Volvo B58-61, Plaxton Supreme IV.

This coach was delivered to Astons late December 1979 and entered service in January 1980.

Photo taken at Astons Yard, Kempsey, September 1980

VAB 100V
Volvo B58-61, Plaxton Supreme IV.
Purchased new in February 1980 and later sold in July 1982 to Baker of Biddulph.
Photo taken at Astons Yard, Kempsey, August 1980

TNP 7V
Volvo, Chassis No13851, Unicar VV6, C57F.
This coach was purchased new in January 1980 and later sold to Jones Caelloi of Pwhelli.
Photo taken at Hillary Road, Worcester, March 1980

VNP 222V

Volvo B58-61, Chassis No13853, Caetano Alpha, C57F.

Purchased new by Astons in March 1980 and sold to Gibson of Moffat in 1982.

Photo taken at Astons Yard, Kempsey, March 1980

LHL 374W

Volvo B10M-61, Chassis No 768 Caetano Alpha, C50Ft.

This coach was new to Belmont of Askern, in May 1981 and joined Astons fleet in July 1982. It was sold in March 1985 to Irvine of Law.

Photo taken at Astons Yard, Kempsey

BNP 5W

Volvo B58-61, Chassis No16349 Plaxton Supreme IV C57F.

Purchased new in February 1981 and later in May 1983 it was sold to Dodsworth of Boroughbridges.

Photo taken at Astons Yard, Kempsey

BNP 11W

Volvo B58-61, Caetano Alpha.

This coach was purchased new in January 1981 and was in the livery of Viking Tours. It was later sold in February 1984 to Leons of Stratford.

Photo taken at Astons Yard, Kempsey

BAB 888W

Volvo B58-61, Chassis No16455 Plaxton Supreme IV, C57F.

Purchased new in 1981 and sold in July 1983 to Mainwaring of Tonyrefail.

Photo taken at Astons Yard, Kempsey

GBB 522K

Leyland Atlantean, Alexander H78F.

This double decker was new to the Tyne and Wear fleet in 1972 and arrived at Astons in February 1981. As all other ex-service double decker's, it was mainly used for school and college contracts.

Photo taken 4th July 1985

WNT 662H

Leyland Atlantean, Alexander H78D.

Again, ex-Tyne and Wear and used mainly for school and college contracts. This bus was used for several years and was sold for scrap to Wacton of Bromyard in 1985.

Photo taken at Astons Yard, Kempsey, August 1982

FAB 333X

Daf, Bova Europa C49FF.

This coach was purchased new in August 1981 and was sold in March 1982 to Wallace Arnold (Devon).

Photo taken at Astons yard

KUY 441X

Volvo, B58-61, Chassis No16165, Van Hool Alizee.
Purchased new in March 1982 and sold to Barry of Cork in April 1984.

Photo taken at Astons Yard, Kempsey, June 1983

KUY 442X

Volvo B58-61, Plaxton Supreme IV, C53F.
Purchased new in March 1982 and sold in September 1985 to Jones of Newchurch.

Photo taken at Astons Yard, Kempsey, June 1983

KUY 443X

Volvo B58-61, Chassis No14392, Duple Dominant 2, C57F.

Purchased new to Astons in July 1982 and sold to Jennings of Bude in May 1985.

Photo taken at Sansome Street, Worcester, June 1983

KUY 444X

Man, Chassis No YE281500A02M14231, Van Hool Acron, C49Ft.

Purchased new in July 1982, sold and exported to Cyprus in 1985.

Photo taken at Astons Yard, Kempsey

BAG 201X

Volvo B58-56, Chassis No 16774, Plaxton Supreme IV, C53F.

Purchased new by Astons in March 1982 and later sold to Jones of Macclefield in October 1986.

Photo taken at Bromyard Road, Worcester

FHS 723X

Volvo B10M-61, Chassis No 3390 Duple Dominant III / Goldliner III, C51Ft.

This coach was new to Parks of Hamilton in April 1982. The coach was one of a batch purchased by Astons in February 1985. This one was sold on to Catterall of Southam in March 1985.

Photo taken at Astons Yard, Kempsey, February 1985

BUS 653K

Volvo B58-56 Chassis No326 Alexander Y type C49F.

This vehicle was the first Volvo PSV in the country, originally a Volvo demonstrator of 1972. Its first owner was Parks of Hamilton and later Trathens of Yelverton. The vehicle was then purchased by Astons from Trathens in October 1978. It ran for a while doing mainly school contract work. It was then decided to have the body removed, which is thought to have been carried out by students at Evesham college. Chassis alterations were carried out extending it to 12 metres and then sent to Van Hool to be fitted with a Alizee body. It was then re-registered with registration number THU 864.

Photos taken at Astons Yard, Kempsey.

OUJ 479X

Ford R1114, Plaxton Supreme IV, C53F.

This coach was purchased by Astons from Price of Wrockwardine in March 1983. It was later sold on to Sunbeam of Hevingham in October 1984.

Photo taken at Sidbury, Worcester, April 1983

A125 SNH

Volvo B10M, Jonckheere Jubilee P90.

It was new to Bakers Dolphin of Weston Super Mare in 1983 and ran with them for about a year. It was then purchased by Astons in 1984. The coach eventually ended up with Thandi Coaches of Smethwick during the early 2000s with the registration number SJI 5616.

Photo taken at Astons Yard, Kempsey

TNP 615Y
Volvo B10m61 Chassis No4702. Duple Laser C57F.
New to Astons in March 1983.
Sold to Stonehouse of Brottton in December 1985.

Photo taken in the yard February 1984

A216 YAB
Volvo B1OM-10 Chassis No 5862 Duple Caribbean C55F.
New to Astons in May 1984, then passed to Smith of Wilmcote and later to Evergreen of Blackheath where it later became JGL 11.

Photo taken at Astons Yard, Kempsey

A215 YAB
Bova EL28-581 Chassis No 2429 Duple Calypso C49FT.
New in May 1984. Sold to Galloway of Mendlesham in March 1986.
Photo taken at Astons Yard, Kempsey

A217 YAB
Bova EL28-581 Chassis No 2446. Duple Calypso C49FT.
New in May 1984. Sold to Caygill of Knaresborough in Jan 1986.
Photo taken in Sansome Walk, Worcester

A734 CUY
Volvo B10M-61 Chassis No 6001 Duple Caribbean C55F.
New in May 1984.
Photo taken at Astons Yard, Kempsey

DWB 269X
Fiat Chassis No 300067 Moseley C18F.
Ex Billies of Mexborough in Nov 1983 Sold to Moon of Shepshed in June 1984.
Photo taken at Astons Yard, Kempsey

DWA 22X
MAN Chassis No 001383. Rebur C27F Body.
Ex Globe of Barnsley in January 1985. Sold to Mullover & G of Goldington in August 1985.
Photo taken at Astons Yard, Kempsey

B876 HWP
Bova Chassis N0 3197 C49FT.
New in April 1985. Re-registered HYY 3 In December 1988.
Photo taken at Astons Yard, Kempsey

Conclusion

So, we come to the end of our pictorial history of a small coach operator in a Worcestershire village. Starting in the 1920s when L.J.(Joe) Aston started with the business of transporting vegetables to the early morning markets, returning to take local children to school, usually in the same vehicle, the truck having an early style of demountable body. This developed through the years, including war time to the 1960s when Joe retired and sold the business to the Halford family. This then developed into a company operating 22 vehicles, travelling around Europe. We conclude our history in the 1980s when those involved moved to other occupations.

Over the latter years a huge variety of models of coach were being operated, including many being the first to be sold in Britain. These included the Bova and Van Hools, some stayed for long periods, others just for weeks. Also, the first coaches with TVs and toilets to be operated in the area. All kinds of work were carried out, from school contracts through to Continental tours. The company is still operating, though not from Kempsey and has now grown to a large operation.

We must pass on our thanks to all those who have given us photographs, mostly ex-employees, but especially Terry Jones for the use of his collection. Also, to members of the Aston family, one of whom is involved with this history for providing pictures from early years of the business.

Bill and Chris Halford

Tony Halford. "Keeping his eye on things"

NUX 109G

Bedford VAM70 Chassis No460233 Duple Viceroy, C45F.

This coach was new to Whittle of Highley, Shropshire.
It arrived at Astons in April 1971 and ran until February 1972 when it passed to Raff of Gravesend, Kent.

Below is a sketch which was given to Trevor Underwood who was the regular driver of NUX 109G in the early 1970s.
It is remembered to have been sketched by a pupil from Hanley Castle Grammar School on a school trip.
At the end of the trip, it was presented to Trevor.